Dedication and Definitions

To the memory of Russell, my brother and soulmate.

Pa • cif • ic, *noun,* largest ocean in the world;

2) adj. calm; tranquil; mild; peaceful.

Soul, *noun,* the seat of human personality, intellect, will, and emotions;

2) noun, the essential part or fundamental nature of anything.

Contents

Preface

As I sit on the magnificent California coast writing this preface to a book I've been compiling for two years, I may be the only person within 500 miles hoping that today's clear, warm weather will yield to dense fog. My gloomy wish for grayer days stems from the fact that the last photograph I need to complete this volume must capture the mystery of a foggy morning. I have already dedicated a page to fog, one of the coast's defining moods, but it lacks an illustration. After staring at the blank fog page for hours, I have concluded that an empty white scene comes close, but just doesn't suffice. It might work for a chapter on snow, but not for the coastal fog that shifts time into slow motion, buffers the sight of trees reaching over rocky cliffs, and mutes the din of sea lions barking in the distance. If tomorrow a dense mist were to shroud the coast, I would grab my camera gear and get an early, anxious start on the day while my neighbors bemoaned the end of a balmy dry spell. Changing weather is one of many variables that affect my seaside moods, reminding me of the deep connection I feel with the Pacific coast.

It is this connection, the sense of the Pacific intertwined with my spirit, that inspired me to combine photography and writing to explore an amazing natural world. The resulting collection is a visual and lyrical journey that reflects the diversity and magnificence of the Pacific coast. It ranges from Mexico's Baja Peninsula, with a whale's eye view of a calving lagoon, to the nocturnal beauty of kayaking under a full moon on a calm California estuary, and on to the perspective of a bald eagle looking down on a fleet of fin whales in Alaska. It shares a sublime encounter with brown bears nursing their cubs and teaching them to dig for clams.

It includes the birth of a harbor seal, its first swig of mother's milk, its first ocean swim, and its well-earned first nap.

This compilation also includes photographs and stories that relate personal encounters with ten endangered species. Several are on their way to recovery; others may not be around for the next generation. Life here teeters on the edge, striking a precarious balance — one that we must be diligent to maintain or, in some cases, restore.

The Pacific coast offers endless surprises. For me, they began when I set out in the spring of 1991 to make a sound financial investment in a house on the Sonoma coast. I was astonished by how quickly the financial venture became a deep emotional investment in the region, its striking landscapes and vibrant wildlife. Small revelations emerged with every outing. One morning in May I ventured to the Kruse Rhododendron Preserve five miles south of my new home, hoping to photograph delicate pink blossoms; instead, I spent the morning mesmerized by the sunlight hitting a fiery red tiger lily that had popped up from the lush forest floor. Incredulity silenced me one afternoon in Alaska as I set out to photograph a hillside of blue lupine and discovered a brown bear and her cub approaching over the crest. I sat motionless while they sauntered by just twenty yards above me.

Unpredictable and unexpected encounters are what make the coast so fascinating. The emerging light of a sunrise can feel like magic. A bold brown pelican may swoop down on my kayak and try to take a bite out of the stern. A great blue heron may wait on a riverbank for a harbor seal to deliver its meal, or a curious seal may brush against the underside of my boat and nibble on its bow.

Anne Chadwick

On this precious segment of North America's West Coast, the longer one sits quietly and watches, the more one sees, hears and feels. The rhythms of nature can silence the static of a busy life. The ocean's shifting scenes, fresh smells, and salty air have a way of washing away day-to-day tensions.

The random placement of this book's stories and illustrations is as dynamic and diverse as a river flowing to the Pacific, twisting and turning, pausing in eddies, tumbling over obstacles, picking up speed, and heading ultimately for the sunset. The collection provides only a brief glimpse into an amazing world where the meeting of sea and land takes on a remarkable array of characteristics – delicate, robust, bold, touching, graceful, ferocious, serene, and striking. One day soon the elusive fog may provide the setting for a photograph that will complete this book, but the journey of discovery will continue.

As I walk along the beach at sunrise I often see animal tracks from the previous night. Raccoons, with their small feet and long toes, frequent the shores under cover of darkness. The narrow hooves of deer leave distinctive prints in the sand going right down to the water, and while I've never seen them swim in the ocean, I've heard they bathe in salt water to wash away fleas.

The great blue heron leaves a nearly straight row of four-toed prints. The slender rear toe faces backward for stability. Without it, the gangly bird might just tip over. Occasionally, I find tracks that look like they were left by a little dog. Perhaps they were, but my imagination pictures a small gray fox or a bobcat. The cats' prints have no claw marks because their claws are retractable, but a canine leaves marks showing distinct claws. At a run, claw marks may be all the shy fox leaves behind.

I savor all the fresh prints on the beach as day breaks, knowing that the next high tide will wipe the sandy canvas clean.

A few days on the Pacific coast could make even the soundest sleeper a morning person. Sunrise emerges as a magical time, creating an intense light that brings a hushed world to attention. On America's western shores the sun rises at the ocean-gazer's back, casting its low-angled rays on breaking waves. Daylight peeks over the coastal range onto water, rocks, and sand. The scene evolves from muted grays to saturated hues in what feels like no time.

Absent a storm, there is rarely any wind at sunrise. Overnight, the differences in temperature and pressure that arise between sea and land, coast and inland, have a chance to equalize, bringing a magnificent calm to the shore.

On several mornings I have seen flocks of pelicans arrive just as first light dances off the waves. Seagulls, the scavengers of the sea, follow at a short distance. A group of California sea lions, some jumping high out of the water, head north just past the cresting waves.

Sanderlings scurry across the sand, darting just beyond the surf's reach to snatch up mollusks and crustaceans exposed by the waves. These diminutive shorebirds spend most of the day zipping up and down the sand in rhythm with the waves, logging miles like marathoners in an endless series of tiny steps.

2- Anne Chadwick

Pelicans

"A wonderful bird is the pelican, his bill can hold more than his belly can."
— Dixon Lanier Merritt

Merritt's limerick speaks the truth: the pouch suspended from the lower half of the pelican's long, straight bill really can hold three times more than its stomach. Pelicans are spectacular fliers, an avian air force maneuvering in single-file formation inches above the ocean. Their fishing technique involves breathtaking dives from heights of up to seventy-five feet. Using their keen eyesight to spot prey from high aloft, they tuck their seven-foot wingspans into their bodies to dive-bomb unsuspecting catch. The pelican's dramatic dive is a common sight because the large birds consume up to four pounds of fish a day.

That's where the infamous beak comes in, scooping up water and fish, and then allowing the water to drain out. Opportunistic seagulls lurk nearby, like hyenas drawn to a lion's kill, hoping for leftovers. The seagulls wait to catch any fish that might escape with the draining water, but pelicans rarely let any fish wriggle free. The pouch can also serve as a cooling mechanism in hot weather, and as a feeding trough for young pelicans, which eat their parents' regurgitated grub.

The brown pelican that graces the Pacific coast has been on the Endangered Species List since 1970. It was the pesticide DDT that drove them toward extinction. It got into the food chain and caused the birds to lay eggs with shells so thin they broke during incubation. Since the United States banned the use of DDT, nesting success has been on the rise. In 1985, the Atlantic population recovered enough to be removed from the endangered list in the eastern United States. The other populations, located in the U.S. Gulf coast, Pacific coast, Central and South America, remain endangered. Recovery is slow because a nesting pair produces only one egg each year.

Pelicans may be too bold for their own good, lacking a healthy distrust of humans. I've had them approach my kayak, and one bird actually chased my boat, opened his enormous beak, and chomped down on the stern. He shook his head, apparently deciding that a plastic boat was not a tasty bite.

When I returned to shore, several boys were playing on the beach and a brave pelican stood nearby. It may have been the same bold creature that played *Jaws* with my boat. One quiet boy edged closer to the bird, which showed interest in the youngster. By the time I had packed up my gear, the boy had befriended the pelican and squatted next to it, trying to mimic its stance. He placed his outstretched fingers on the sand in front of him to imitate the bird's webbed feet. He craned his neck, squinted his eyes, and put on a sweet smile. With his short-cropped blond hair, he did manage to take on a certain likeness to the creature. I took their picture and asked if the bird had a name.

"I call him Melville," the boy said. "He's my friend."

The Audubon Society says the brown pelican has a history of at least 30 million years. It would be a shame to end it on our watch.

4 Anne Chadwick

Elephant Seals

One spring a lone elephant seal showed up in the middle of a harbor seal rookery along the Sonoma coast in mid-April and stayed for four weeks. The harbor seals gave her a wide berth, and each time I got downwind I figured her unfortunate odor was responsible for the large amount of real estate they granted her. She was molting and smelled like rotting flesh. Elephant seals normally congregate in a few huge colonies along the California coast, most notably Año Nuevo State Reserve near Santa Cruz, where more than 2,000 seals gather each winter for breeding and birthing.

Each year they do a massive and catastrophic molt, and often end up with infected lesions or skin disease. The Sonoma stray, a young female, appeared fairly healthy, although she lost weight during the month as molting took its toll on her metabolism. She flipped sand on her back and dug trenches to cool herself, and she took shelter from the full sun by ducking into a driftwood fort that previous beachgoers had constructed. Far more vocal than the quiet harbor

seals, she cackled at seagulls, seals, and human onlookers. She looked out of place among the harbor seals, set apart by her wide head, large body, peeling skin, and foul smell.

She would have been more at home in the colony of elephant seals I had seen near San Simeon on the Central California coast. They all smelled bad. My first visit there was after breeding season, which extends from December through March, and the adult males had left for the open sea. What I saw was probably a group of "weaners," seals who were about a month old. Having fed on their mothers' rich milk, the pups had grown from their birth weight of seventy-five pounds to somewhere between 250 and 350 pounds. I read that some resourceful pups nurse from two or three females. They can weigh 600 pounds and are aptly called "super weaners." I watched a few hefty juveniles practice fighting techniques that would later determine which bull controlled the best territory and the largest harem.

At Año Nuevo one January I witnessed the spectacle of adult males bashing each other with their gigantic necks in a bloody battle for dominance. The bulls' broad chests and necks sported enormous scars from past confrontations. Watching the adult males, it was obvious how they got the elephant name: they had large snouts that drooped over their muzzles. During mating season their snouts inflate, curving down and back into their mouths. The huge bulls, up to twenty-one feet long and weighing two-and-a-half tons, have been recorded diving more than 5,000 feet deep, staying underwater for an hour and a half. I always wondered what an enormous animal with that much blubber would look like under the pressure of a 5,000-foot dive—probably long and skinny like a giant squid, one of its favorite foods.

Elephant seals spend 80 percent of their lives in the open sea, and nearly all of that is spent underwater eating, sleeping, digesting and travelling. Their bodies undergo remarkable transformations enabling them to survive at depths that would squeeze the life out of any other mammal. Their heart rates drop from between 55 and 120 beats per minute on land to 4 to 15 beats per minute at depth. They carry all the oxygen needed for diving in their blood, rather than in their lungs. Before they dive, elephant seals exhale and collapse their lungs, and the blood flow to their extremities drops to nearly nothing.

Males and females take separate vacations, in a sense. The males' semiannual migration takes them to the Aleutian Islands, while females feed in the northeast Pacific and near Hawaii. Their two-pronged migrations add up to about 12,000 miles a year.

In the 1890s these seals were nearly exterminated by the whaling industry, which went after their great rolls of blubber to be rendered for oil. In 1892 a tiny colony of fewer than fifty animals was discovered on Guadalupe Island, off Baja, California. The Mexican government gave protected status to the elephant seal, and the U.S. government followed suit a couple of years later. The population now numbers about 160,000, which breed on offshore islands from Baja to San Francisco. The growing population pushed the seal's habitat back to the mainland, with the first modern birth in California recorded in 1975. By 1979, almost a hundred cows had given birth at the Año Nuevo rookery, and in 2002, an estimated 2,000 gave birth on the mainland. Their range now spreads from the Gulf of Alaska to Baja, where the population appears to thrive.

Like harbor seals, the elephant seals mate a few weeks after giving birth, around the time of weaning. Both species experience a rare phenomenon known as "delayed implantation," in which the fertilized egg does not implant in the wall of the uterus for several months. The theory is that the female is so weak after nursing that she can't nourish the egg.

The elephant seal colonies I've seen are noisy and active, while the harbor seals are quiet and placid. Harbor seals rarely interact other than to mate, and they really don't like to touch each other. If touched, they growl, snort, scratch, bite, or butt the personal-space invader with their heads. Elephant seals, in contrast, think nothing of walking right over each other. In fact, the 5,000-pound males sometimes kill babies by crushing them to get where they're going.

The lone elephant seal in the harbor seal rookery disappeared after about a month on the beach and likely took to the open water for several months. She may have found a colony headed north to bulk up on an abundance of fish, squid, and octopus. She and her companions would feed off the coast of northern Washington and Vancouver Island in British Columbia and would not appear on land again until September. I doubted I would ever see her again.

Wild Azaleas

A hiker might smell them before seeing them. Wild azaleas emit a delicious, spicy fragrance that induces deep inhaling and broad smiles under closed eyes. In Oregon they are called honeysuckle, probably due to the sweet aroma, but their scientific name is Western Azalea *(Rhododendron occidentale.)*

These enormous shrubs with their fabulous flowers thrive in seepage areas and stream banks. When I approached to photograph a ten-foot-tall azalea bush in a coastal meadow, I nearly lost a hiking boot to the bog. This azalea on the Sonoma coast began blooming in April, and the yellow-orange accents on pale pink petals evoked the image of Easter eggs snatched up by anxious children rushing to fill their baskets.

In nature a plant this showy and fragrant has to have a defense mechanism, for it certainly draws the attention of hungry browsers. High toxicity keeps the wild azalea safe from nibbling deer, sheep, and cattle.

10- Anne Chadwick

Late in the spring of 1991 I decided to buy a house on the Sonoma coast. The first real estate agent to show me around was an older man with white hair and a flushed complexion who kept saying, "What's a little gal like you going to do all by herself up here in these woods?" *Little gal like me?* Did he not notice that I was five-feet-nine with the ideal build to play small forward in basketball?

He wanted to show me properties adjacent to the golf course. Apparently, he had me pegged as the country-club type. He also thought I would be most interested in houses with a lot of closet space, "because I know how you gals can fill up a closet." Maybe he didn't see that I was wearing worn- out jeans, hiking boots, and an old workshirt that was a hand-me-down from my big brother. Two days in a row.

As we rolled up to one house I spotted a beautiful buck, his handsome rack of antlers looming over tall grass. "Wish I had my gun," he said, holding the deer in his imaginary sights. I couldn't wait to get out of his car and find another agent.

With the help of a new agent, I managed to find a small fixer-upper in a sunny clearing in the redwoods. Over the years I have seen an endless parade of wildlife pass through the property, including quail, wild turkeys, brush rabbits, deer, raccoons, and the occasional skunk.

In the spring of 2002 a doe wandered past my window with her two newborn fawns, still wobbly and sporting the spots of a baby. As the year progressed I watched them grow. Their little bodies gained strength, and muscles appeared under coats that gradually lost their spots. On their daily journey through my yard I noticed the youngsters gaining confidence, wandering farther from their mother as time went on. I was particularly pleased when the young fawns finally decided that my so-called deer-resistant landscaping wasn't worth sampling on their way through.

Egrets

Egrets confuse me. When I see a beautiful white bird on long legs, I admire it but don't always know whether I'm appreciating a snowy egret, great egret, cattle egret, or the white form of a great blue heron.

I enjoy seeing and even trying to identify the Pacific coast's enormous variety of birds, but I am not a fanatical birdwatcher. One time on the west shore of San Juan Island I was thrilled to witness a pod of orcas swim by close to the rocky coast. A few minutes latter a gaggle of British birdwatchers appeared over the rocks, out of breath and trembling with excitement.

"Did you see it?" one asked, pressing enormous binoculars against his ruddy cheeks.

"Yes, I love it when the orcas swim by so close to shore," I said.

"No, no," he shook his head. "The duck."

These birdwatchers had come all the way from England to see one rare duck, whose name I don't even recall. They were oblivious to the killer whales that lurked in nearby waters. I'm not that kind of birdwatcher, just a casual observer.

One crisp January morning on the Monterey Peninsula a small white bird caught my eye. No bigger than a nearby seagull, this little fellow had shaggy white feathers and distinctive legs that sported black fronts and yellow backs. *The National Geographic Field Guide to Birds of North America* has a wonderful illustration of a juvenile snowy egret with just those legs. It says they use their legs to stir up prey in shallow water and then stab at it with their black beaks.

On another visit to Monterey, I admired a much larger white bird that stood perfectly still in the morning sun,

perched on one long black leg. Like a great heron, he had four toes that left intriguing tracks in sand, with three long, clawed toes pointing forward and the fourth headed straight back for stability. When I looked him up in the bird book, his yellow bill set him apart from the snowy egret, and his black legs indicated he was not one of those sneaky white great blue herons, so I took him for a great egret. Black cormorants stood at attention on each side of this stately fellow, creating a perfect contrast in color and style.

14- Anne Chadwick

Waves

The ocean's shifting scenes, fresh smells, and salty air have a calming effect on my soul. The sea washes away my water-soluble tensions; rhythmic waves put me in a meditative trance, and there are new discoveries on every outing.

After a storm the air may be clear, but violent waves pound the shore, a reminder of what unsettled weather can do to an enormous body of water like the Pacific. The overwhelming power and beauty of a heaving sea on rocky shores make me shout with excitement. I stand at the edge of Black Point, thirty-five feet above the sea, where the spray drenches me, even at that height. The taste of saltwater on my lips makes them curl upward in delight.

John Muir wrote about water as an animate object, its "furies, screaming, hissing, and surging… a perfect hell of conflicting demons." When the roar of a wave crashing against a rocky cliff rattles my body, I understand why he called them living waters.

After a storm the sun streaks through dissipating clouds to light the swells. With the sun at my back I see a rainbow in the mist that lingers over the crest of each wave.

I retreat from Black Point on a trail that crosses a natural bridge, and listen to the sea surging through a tunnel below. One day the mighty water will wash away this bridge, leaving a new sea stack for future generations to admire from a redefined shore.

16- Anne Chadwick

Sea Otters

I usually hear sea otters before I see them. Their use of tools gives them away, as they smash open shells against rocks that rest on their table-hard stomachs. One of the only marine mammals to use tools, they also make use of various objects to pry prey from underwater rocks. Their dexterity is due in part to the fact that they have paws, not flippers. They're more closely related to minks than the seals and sea lions with whom they share the water.

I followed the hammering sound one late afternoon near Black Point on the Sonoma coast and was startled to see a California sea otter feeding just beyond the cresting waves. The southern sea otter's range is not supposed to extend north of San Francisco, but there it was, about a hundred miles astray. I took its presence in my neighborhood as a good sign that the fragile population was on the mend. That was in the mid-1990s, but the numbers are declining again – from nearly 2,400 in 1995 to about 2,000 in 2002.

The California population fell to less than twenty toward the end of the 1800s, hunted nearly to extinction because of their splendid fur. I have run my fingers through otter pelts at a couple of museums, and they are exquisite. Humans have about 600,000 hairs on their heads; the sea otter has 2 million per square inch. Their dense fur, not blubber, provides insulation against frigid ocean waters.

Back in the early 1800s Russians came to what is now the Sonoma coast in search of sea lion and otter furs. They took 1,000 acres from the Pomo Indians in exchange for three horses, three pairs of breeches, three blankets, two axes, and a handful of beads, and they established Fort Ross. The Russians planted orchards, raised livestock, logged redwoods, and harvested sea otters, nearly depleting them by 1839. When the fur trade dried up, they sold the fort to John Sutter, the Swiss pioneer who had his main fort in Sacramento and discovered gold in his Coloma mill, setting off the Gold Rush of 1849.

Today the sea otter is considered "threatened" under the Endangered Species Act. While the California population struggles, related subspecies in southeast Alaska and Washington are doing quite well. The Aleutian Island population is dramatically declining, and scientists aren't sure why. Perhaps the biggest advantage this smallest of marine mammals has is that humans find it incredibly cute. There's nothing like a fat, furry face (which graces every coffee mug and tee shirt on the Monterey Peninsula) to spark sympathy for this delicate species.

Solitude

"By my intimacy with nature I find myself withdrawn from man. My interest in the sun and the moon, in the morning and the evening, compels me to solitude."
— Henry David Thoreau (1817–1862)

I have walked for miles along sections of the Pacific coast without encountering another human being. The solitude is exquisite. It calms my soul and fosters creativity. The most isolated segments of this magnificent shore seem to satisfy my reclusive tendencies.

I do not equate solitude with loneliness. Instead, it is a delicious luxury. I may sit in a biting wind to see if a sunset will develop vivid colors, and there is no concern that a companion will suffer from cold toes or frozen fingers. I may linger near a bird's nest for hours to see if its occupants will return and give me a glimpse of their intriguing lives. Alone, I respond only to my internal clock, oblivious to external schedules. I sit quietly and let the rhythms of nature silence the drumbeat of societal pressures.

French Renaissance writer Michel de Montaigne (1533-1592), in his essay *On Solitude* said, "We must reserve a back shop all our own, entirely free, in which to establish our real liberty and our principal retreat and solitude." The beach has become my back shop, the place I go to unwind, regroup, and regain perspective.

In the wilderness, I know that even without a person in sight, I am not alone. As I stroll a deserted cove, an osprey watches from a cliff high above. Nimble sanderlings dart in and out of the surf. A harbor seal lifts its head above the waves to follow my movement across an otherwise isolated beach.

Fin Whales

I knew from the first blow that the whales swimming near our boat on Alaska's Katmai Coast were extraordinarily large. Their spouts shot to a height of twenty-five feet, much taller than grays' or humpbacks', indicating enormous lung capacity. The only time I had seen such a blow was a rare blue whale sighting off the Sonoma coast. The whales in Alaska's Shelikof Straight were fin whales, second in size to only the blue whale. In all likelihood these fin whales were much bigger than our comfortable sixty-five-foot boat, as adult males measure up to seventy-eight feet in the northern hemisphere, and eighty-eight feet in the southern hemisphere. Populations from each hemisphere remain distinct because northern fin whales never meet their southern counterparts.

Our boat's captain slowed to admire the enormous creatures, and we watched them surface a few times before they disappeared into the depths. Their immense backs seemed extremely broad, yet our view equated to the proverbial tip of the iceberg. Our surface view provided only a tiny glimpse of their long, sleek bodies that are streamlined to place them among the fastest of the great whales. They can sprint up to twenty-three miles per hour, earning them the nickname "greyhound of the sea."

The fin whales that we admired from the boat used their tremendous speed in what seemed a lopsided game of hide-and-seek, very much in their favor as they changed direction underwater and reappeared far from the boat. They may have been feeding on krill or chasing a school of small fish. They have been observed circling schools of fish at high speed, rolling the fish into compact balls, then turning on their right sides to engulf the fish. They can consume up to two tons of fish a day, a reasonable fraction of their total body weight, fifty to seventy tons.

It wasn't until my flight across the Shelikof Straight in a small floatplane that I saw the most unusual characteristic of fin whales. The coloring of their lower jaws is asymmetrical, white or creamy yellow on the right side and mottled black on the left. The unique coloring no doubt serves a purpose, probably providing camouflage for the great fish round-up.

The aerial view of a veritable fleet of fin whales, spouting in unison, was unforgettable. Although they are found in all oceans of the world, their speed and preference for vast open seas make them a rare sight. The present populations are estimated to be about 40,000 in the northern hemisphere and there may be as many as 20,000 in the southern hemisphere, a small percentage of original population levels. As many as 30,000 fin whales were slaughtered each year from 1935 to 1965, before the International Whaling Commission placed them under full protection. I felt privileged to see a handful during my Alaskan travels.

22- Anne Chadwick

Rhododendrons

The Pacific coast's wild rhododendrons seem almost reluctant to bloom. They wait until most other plants have put on their spring show, and then they send out fabulous blossoms, delicate and pale pink. The colorful blooms stand out against lush green forests where they thrive. Their name comes from the Greek *rhodon* (rose) and *dendron* (tree), very fitting as the gnarly shrubs often grow to the height of trees.

The rhododendrons I see in California's coastal forests are tall, spindly plants. They stretch up twenty-five feet, and although they will never out-compete their towering redwood neighbors for sunlight, they try. The roots reach into moist soil made acidic by fallen pine needles. They are so well suited to the redwoods that a plant can actually take root in the decaying stump of a fallen giant.

Their flowers almost glow on damp, foggy days. When the fog lifts, they soak up the sun's filtered rays, which stretch through redwoods to create a cathedral's light. I am humbled to stroll their magnificent territory, breathe the air we share with giant ferns, listen to the wind through ancient branches, and smell the wet soil and thick moss. I stop to enjoy the forest's stillness, and hear water tumbling over polished rocks. The grace and grandeur of these rhododendrons bowl me over.

Great Blue Herons

Great blue herons wade in shallow waters, gangly on legs like stilts. They lurch through native grasses, standing more than four feet high. They become nearly invisible when they stand motionless, ready to strike at unsuspecting prey. Taking flight, awkward at first then graceful in the air, they stretch enormous wings and fold their long necks back to their shoulders.

One afternoon while paddling on the Big River, near Mendocino, I spotted a heron on the riverbank. He stretched his long slender neck, counterbalancing his gray and white body over stick-like legs. He waded into shallow water near the bank and then froze to hide from prey. Steady as a rock, his lack of movement piqued my curiosity. A harbor seal approached. Surely, I thought, the heron isn't stalking the seal.

The seal dived under my kayak. I floated, motionless, and watched. When the seal resurfaced, dozens of small fish—probably herring—jumped out of the water in a last-ditch effort to escape the seal's fierce jaws. One of the unfortunate fish flew right up out of the water, evading the seal, but ending up in the heron's waiting beak. The wily heron had simply waited on the banks for the seal to deliver a meal, which popped nearly straight into the wading bird's mouth.

My friend Sandy shared another story that proved the heron's extraordinary avian IQ. She stood on a Sea Ranch bluff watching seals bask in the sun when a great blue heron caught her attention.

"It was the one that stomps around on the bluff path and through the iris field," she said. She had seen him often and learned that he would stand his ground if she approached calmly and did not make eye contact. "He dug and dug and poked and poked until he came up with a huge snake in his beak." She described the snake as all one color, as big around as a fifty-cent piece, and long enough to hang from the heron's beak with both its head and its tail touching the ground.

"That would make it about eight feet long?" I asked.

"Yes, about that," she continued. "The heron tried for a while to reposition the snake, but the snake kept striking at his breast feathers." Then the crafty bird hopped up and flew down to the water's edge with the snake wriggling in his beak. After working his beak closer to the snake's head, the heron held the snake underwater until it drowned. "Then began the swallow process," she said. "I didn't have an hour to watch, so as he started to swallow, I left."

26- Anne Chadwick

Full Moon

When the moon is full, it rises exactly opposite the setting sun. On those evenings I can almost feel a lunar surge in my veins, drawing me out to meet the rising tide. One October afternoon just before sunset, I took my kayak to the mouth of the Gualala River, which spills out of steep wooded canyons to meet the sea. As I pointed the kayak upstream into the forest, the setting sun reflected orange and pink off the water. Magnificent redwoods glowed in the fading light. The river turned the color of honey and it felt warm dripping off the paddle onto my hands. I caught sight of two river otters playing near the banks. I paused, watching their sleek bodies roll, flip, and slap the water, until they disappeared into the underbrush. I tracked them with my ears, listening to them devour a fish carcass and then scurry up the bank, out of earshot.

Farther upstream, after several bends in the river, I came into a wide valley facing southeast. A hush fell on the river, the silence broken only by the rush of air through the wings of a red hawk overhead. The sun lit just the tops of the highest trees when I noticed a glow emerging behind them. A few minutes passed before a yellow moon peeked over the ridge, enormous against distant redwoods. I turned to paddle downstream as moonlight knifed through the branches and my kayak sliced in silence through inky water.

As I neared the ocean, where waves pushed saltwater into the fresh flow, seals floated in the river's mouth, fixing their enormous eyes on mine. The water had turned to glass. Moonlight danced on the ripples that grew from each side of my kayak's pointed nose. The full moon filled the sky with magic.

28- Anne Chadwick

Curious Pup

I never tire of watching seal pups, from the moment they're born in the spring until they reach nearly full size by autumn. By July most pups on the northern California coast are weaned and independent, hanging out like teenagers with their peers to forage, fish, and play games. They chase each other, do flips, slap their tails on the water, and dart around in an underwater ballet. The sea is so clear that, even from the bluffs, I can spy them swimming upside down, their white bellies flying a foot or two under the water.

One July afternoon I took my kayak to a very protected inlet on the Sonoma coast. With the bow pointed straight into modest waves, I waited for a surge to lift my boat off the sand. I scooted forward, paddled hard, and punched through to calmer water beyond the shore break. I braced against the cold spray, a stark contrast to my body's warmth, which I guarded vigilantly under layers of neoprene, fleece, and a wind jacket. I tensed against the ocean's powerful movements, fearful that a wave would overtake me. But as the swells became gentle and rhythmic, I was able to relax into the cadence of paddling around the cove, letting my grip loosen around the shaft. I relaxed my hips and let the swells lead me around the ocean's dance floor.

My strokes stopped when I spotted a small pup approaching. By his size and round face I guessed he was about two months old, born in late April or early May. At first he kept a distance of about thirty feet, but he seemed very curious. He looked at me, ducked under the water, came up a little closer, and gazed at me some more. He began swimming under my boat, and through the clear water I could see him ten or twelve feet beneath me. I saw his eyes peering up at me from below on each pass.

He surfaced closer to the boat each time. He popped up ten feet away, then did some somersaults, tried a few barrel rolls under me, and came up about six feet away. Then he surfaced just six inches from the front of my boat and locked eyes with me. I didn't budge, except to let my smile grow wider each time he came nearer. My heart raced, not from fear, but from the exhilaration of being so near this wild pup.

The little guy made a few more passes under my boat and then started nuzzling the bow. I couldn't tell if he was sucking or chewing on it, but I felt the vibration of his mouth against the boat. He also used his flippers to feel the hull. Then he went back underwater, belly up, and rubbed against the plastic again and again. When he surfaced, his huge brown eyes sparkled and his silvery coat glistened in the sun.

A couple of times, when the pup approached my kayak from underneath, I reached in and stroked his belly as he swam by. Tears ran down my cheeks when I felt his soft, sleek coat. He stayed next to me in the water and let me rub his body. I thought he would be afraid, but I was the one with the fear. He put his flipper on my arm, and I instinctively pulled away when I felt his long claws.

Tide Pools

When I was a young child, my mother taught me that the key to appreciating a tide pool is serenity. One lazy summer afternoon she pointed me toward the shallow pools of seawater that lined Shaw's Cove at Laguna Beach, a slice of paradise in Southern California.

"There's nothing in there," I whined.

"Be patient," she advised. "The longer you sit quietly and watch, the more you'll see."

In what seemed like an epic battle against the impatience of youth, I sat and waited for movement. Nothing budged. I poked at dark purple mussels lining one side of the pool, attached fiercely to the rocks and apparently to each other. I was not impressed.

"Sit still," Mom urged. "You'll see."

When I stopped fidgeting, several anemones opened and

their stubby gray-green tentacles swayed with the swell. Unable to keep my hands to myself, I stuck my tiny finger in an anemone's mouth and felt its tentacles tighten around me.

"Sit on your hands," she said. It was a trick she often used to keep my brothers from pestering each other in the back seat on long car trips, and it proved effective at tide pool's edge, as well. Waves washed over an orange sea star clinging to a rock. A small red crab, about the size of my little fist, made its way through the shallow pool. Then a larger wave washed in a small octopus, its suctioned tentacles dancing in the water. With the next wave the slimy creature scooted back out to deeper water.

Before long I noticed movement from several small shells. Hermit crabs poked their tiny pincers out from under their mobile homes and scurried across the rocks. Mom declared my sit-on-your-hands sentence fully served, and she showed me how to pick up a small shell, put some seawater in the palm of my hand and place the delicate crab there. It had fully retracted, but—again with the patience—I held perfectly still until it emerged. Its fine, blue-tipped legs tickled my skin. As darkness fell, my mother had to drag me away from the fascinating oceanic world I had discovered through new-found staying power.

The lessons of patience and quiet observation, which my mother applied both to tide pools and to life in general, have served me well over the years. I still find myself scrambling over slick black rocks, while low-hanging clouds dissect the fiery sun as it approaches the horizon. I sometimes spot a hermit crab retreating into its tiny home, and know that I should return to mine.

Gray Whales

Waves crashed onto a jagged point, sending foam skyward in rhythmic sets. The scene was a French Impressionist painting in motion, changing with the swells and evolving like a Monet study of varying light as the fog came and went and the sun crossed from east to west. A lone gray whale lingered in the bay, sending a spout into the air every few minutes before a deep dive.

Each spring I salute the gray whales passing by the northern California coast on their way from Mexico's calving lagoons to Alaska's feeding grounds. Males and unmated females lead the world's longest mammal migration, while mothers and calves stop to nurse along the way.

Most of what I learned about gray whales came from a week in San Ignacio Lagoon, a bay four miles wide and twenty miles long, on the Pacific coast of Mexico's Baja Peninsula. Each day our guide led half a dozen whale enthusiasts in a *ponga*, a fifteen-foot wooden motorboat, in search of whales who wanted to play. For some reason—maybe the purr of the engine, maybe the funny-looking people onboard—the calves liked to approach the boats. They got so close that we could reach out and touch them while their mothers floated nearby with watchful eyes. The babies' skin was dark, smooth, and rubbery, like a wet inner tube. Adults, on the other hand, were covered with white barnacles and pink parasites that gave them a rough, crusty feel.

We never chased the whales. They chased us. The northern half of San Ignacio Lagoon is a refuge where people and boats are not allowed. One morning as we played with a

calf, the wind pushed us across the boundary, and our guide said we would have to motor south to avoid violating the sanctuary. Our boat pushed gently through the waves and when we looked back to say goodbye to the infant whale and his mother, we saw that they were following us. When we were safely into the southern section, we set the engine to idle and let the calf approach for more playtime.

Gray whales give birth to a single calf, never twins, which makes sense when the baby is a fifteen-foot, 2,000-pound calf that consumes about 150 gallons of fat-laden milk each day. The calf is practically helpless at birth, and his mother supports him at the surface for his first few breaths of air, buoying him up with her own back and flukes. She is very protective and can be aggressive when her calf is in danger. Sitting in the little *ponga*, which was less than one-third the mother's length, I wished I hadn't read the words of Charles Melville Scammon, captain of a whaling ship in the 1850s: "The parent animal, in her frenzy, will chase the boats, and, overtaking them, will overturn them with her head or dash them to pieces with a stroke of her ponderous flukes."

We managed to avoid being dashed to pieces by the ponderous flukes of the thirty-ton mothers, but we got a sense of their size when they breached in the lagoon. No one really knows what motivates a whale to breach. One would suddenly burst from the water, launching its huge body into the air before turning onto its side and crashing into the sea with an enormous splash. Our guide speculated that breaching could be an impressive show of strength meant to lure potential mates, a warning signal to other whales, an attempt to dislodge parasites, or just plain fun.

Some of the youngsters practiced feeding in the lagoon, although scientists say the whales feed only in Alaska – not in the lagoon or on the 10,000-mile migration. In Alaska an adult may regain up to a third of its total body weight. A gray whale feeds by scraping its mouth along the ocean floor, sucking mud off the bottom, and then releasing the mud through its baleen. The food gets trapped on the baleen and scraped off by the whale's thirty-pound tongue. I watched a gray whale feeding in Alaska, leaving a trail of mud after each dive.

Gray whales were removed from the Endangered Species List in 1994 when they recovered to an estimated high of more than 26,000 from near extinction. Hunting nearly erased them from the planet in the mid-1800s. By 1880, so few whales survived that hunting the gray was no longer profitable. Hunters in the eastern Pacific pursued what was left of the gray whales until most nations recognized a treaty that protected the species. I had to laugh when I was eavesdropping on a party of four in a Gualala coffee shop who complained that they couldn't get any reading done because every time they looked up they saw another whale.

Photo by Bill Chadwick

"All day, it was one whale after another!" one coffee drinker said.

An Associated Press article published in May 2002 said that the population of gray whales had dropped in the past four years from an estimated high of more than 26,000 to fewer than 18,000. Scientists speculated that the decline was related to low food supplies in the Arctic feeding grounds, and that the numbers would rise again as climate conditions returned to normal. The article quoted a biologist with the National Marine Fisheries Service, who said the drop could be attributed to a population that had rebounded so well that it had reached the limit of what the environment could sustain. I hope they're right about the population dip being temporary. Personally, I enjoy having my reading interrupted by a steady string of migrating whales.

A Walk in the Redwoods

There's nothing like a walk through ancient redwoods to regain perspective on one's place in this world. Redwood National Park at the upper reaches of California's coastline includes the world's tallest trees. The highest reaches almost 386 feet, enough to cause a six-foot-tall person to develop a serious crick in the neck. Many of the trees in Jedediah Smith Redwoods State Park are between 1,500 and 2,000 years old. I find it difficult to keep my mouth closed while hiking among these giants, since it's usually hanging open in awe, my chin lagging behind as my neck cranes my head upward to peer at the lofty treetops.

But it's important to look down once in a while during a hike through magnificent redwood groves. In early spring, the Western Trillium might be in bloom. A member of the lily family, this elegant three-leafed plant sends up a single white flower about three inches in diameter. It has three petals, which are white at first and turn pink as they age, and three green sepals offset petals.

Also gracing the forest floor may be spectacular mushrooms, which thrive in the moist forest environment. They are fungi, not plants, and do not carry out photosynthesis, so they feed on organic matter, living or dead. One of the most spectacular mushrooms, which is also deadly poisonous, is the Fly Amanita. It stands about five inches tall and its red cap grows to about five inches across. The bright red cap has white warts on top and delicate gills underneath. It is a thing of beauty, and its poisonous nature enables it to grow undisturbed despite its showiness.

Yet another reason to look at the ground once in a while is to avoid stepping on a banana slug. On my first encounter with the slimy gastropod I immediately understood the origin of its name. A good-sized specimen with a yellow body and black spots had climbed to the rim of my garbage can, and I reached out to grab it, thinking someone had tossed a banana peel into the trash and had come up short. I jumped back a couple of feet when I touched its strange, wet body and realized my mistake.

Seal Pups

The Pacific coast can be magnificent any time of year, but the most spectacular season is spring. The air feels so fresh it almost hurts. Spring is pupping season for harbor seals, who establish rookeries where females return each year to give birth and nurse their young on sandy beaches protected by rocky coves. I have spent hour after hour observing seals in one rookery inhabited by about fifty female seals on the Sonoma coast.

One day in April I chuckled as a tiny seal pup discovered that it had a flipper. He looked at it, chewed on it, shook it and hit himself on the head with it. It came in handy to swat away a seagull that approached and tried to peck at the three inches of umbilical cord still hanging off his belly. The cord was one indication that he was just a few days old, and his loose skin was another. The mottled gray skin hung on him like an oversized suit, wrinkled and baggy on his tiny body. Within a week he would fill up on his mother's rich milk and press out the folds with fat and muscle.

Three hugely expectant seals rested by themselves at the south end of that beach, away from the commotion of twenty newborn pups. I settled into a spot on the bluff about twenty feet above the maternity ward and sat motionless to avoid disturbing their peace. Within five minutes, the largest seal started having contractions. She wiggled around a little, but not much, and soon I saw a birth sack begin to emerge between her hind flippers. It appeared translucent and shiny with moisture. Within seconds, the pup's head burst the sack, sending fluid onto the sand, and I saw his little nose and whiskers poke out. Then his entire head and neck emerged, and within about two minutes the pup came all the way out. I held my breath until he took his first

gulp of air and let out a startled cry. The mother turned around and touched her nose to his, initiating the bonding process. The birth had taken less than ten minutes.

During the next few moments this rather large pup, probably at least twenty-five pounds, made many attempts at nursing. The new mother nudged him in the right direction and after several false starts, he latched on to her sandy nipple and wouldn't let go.

The pup nursed for about fifteen minutes before a lone seagull arrived to pester the mother, who eluded the annoying bird by taking her newborn pup into the water.

Pups can swim immediately after birth, yet they are always born on land. I watched this pair swim in the serene cove for about ten minutes before they reappeared on the beach. Both looked healthy and calm, although the silvery new pup barely had enough muscle to pull himself up onto the sand. He looked more at ease in the water. His instinct to nurse remained intact. This time the pup had only a few false starts before finding his mother's teat, full of nutritious milk that would nurture him for six weeks of phenomenal growth. He nursed for several minutes and then pulled away, opened his pink mouth in a wide yawn, and fell asleep beside his mother.

40- Anne Chadwick

42- Anne Chadwick

Birds of Prey

Walt Whitman wrote about the dalliance of eagles, an aerial courtship, claws interlocking, four wings and two beaks tumbling and turning in a freefall. They always pull up at what seems to be the last second. Safe sex it does not appear to be. Many birds of prey perform exuberant, aerobatic mating dances that look more precarious than teenagers with metal braces kissing on a roller coaster. One way or another, they all seem to survive their rituals.

Red-tailed hawks perform another kind of aerial dance, dodging pesky crows and blackbirds who mob them in flight. The hawks, with a wingspan exceeding four feet, are much larger than their haranguers, but they bob and weave to evade their pursuers in midair.

I paused to watch several Northern Harriers patrol a grassy field at Pt. Reyes Seashore one extremely windy afternoon. They flew low over tall grasses, wings raised at an angle, adjusting to each gust with grace. They hovered when they spotted a tasty meal, probably a small rodent. Their diet consists of mice, rats, frogs, and baby birds. The high wind may have complicated their hunting that afternoon, for I did not see a single bird catch a bite to eat.

Golden eagles, with wings reaching up to six-and-a-half feet, are large enough to feed on small mammals such as gray foxes or young bobcats. I have shuddered when one has flown overhead with a snake in its talons, the prey still wriggling in its enormous grasp.

Cormorants

The ocean has a way of washing away the tensions of daily life. Waves often mesmerize me, and new discoveries always astonish me. On one walk I ventured out on a narrow peninsula that reached into a beautiful, secluded cove. Rocky cliffs plunged into turquoise water where two seals floated with the swell. I sat watching the seals and enjoying the quiet.

White streaks lined the cliffs, and, using binoculars, I discovered that the stripes were bird guano below nests perched on impossibly small rock ledges. Before long a cormorant returned to a nest, and I grinned as two tiny heads came to life from within. They reached up to receive a meal from the throat of their mother, a tall, slender bird with black feathers that shone iridescent green and purple in the sunlight. She was a Pelagic cormorant, a bird that nests on ledges so narrow that it must land and take off facing the cliff. The Pelagic cormorant's range is from central California, into the Bering Strait, around the Pacific arc to Japan.

My mother had told me years earlier that Asian fishermen used cormorants to do their job. They placed a ring at the base of the bird's long, slender neck, which enabled the bird to catch a fish and begin to swallow, but prohibited the fish from passing beyond the ring. The fisherman then retrieved the bird and snatched the fish from its neck.

Cormorants' wings, of course, get wet when they dive for fish. Between fishing expeditions cormorants stand on rocks or branches and hold out their wings like washing on a line, taking advantage of the ocean breeze to dry and fluff.

But the mother bird on the cliff was too busy feeding her chicks to pause for the dry cycle. When she left her nest she looked like a diver performing a reverse half somersault, and then descended to her flight path just inches above the sea in search of more food for her little ones.

Raccoons

The French term for raccoon is *raton laveur,* literally washing rat. I always liked the image of the little mammal as an overgrown, albeit fastidious, rodent. In my neighborhood on the northern California coast they're better known as masked bandits.

I awoke one night to find two raccoons inside my brother Russell's van, rifling through bags of groceries, with a bead on the dog food. Making my way downstairs to check on the noise, I found Russell sound asleep in the guest bedroom with his dog, Butch, curled against his legs. When I reached the van, I noticed that a white substance—probably sugar—powdered the nose of one raccoon, which looked right at me and then returned to the task at hand.

"Shoo!" I said with authority, waving my arms as I approached. But they didn't budge. "Scram!" I yelled with even more authority. Not a flinch. "Git, haaaaaaw!" Nothing. These animals had no fear. It took a broomstick and lots of noise to chase them away from the groceries.

The next morning, I asked my brother why he left the van's side door open all night.

"For Butch," he said. "See, if he wants to go outside before I get up, he can run around and then come back to the van for a drink of water or curl up on the seats."

"I thought I noticed a bowl of water in there," I said. There was enough dog hair on every seat, including the driver's, to indicate that Butch had claimed them all.

"My car is just a mobile doghouse for Butch," Russell said. "Tonight it won't be full of groceries, so the raccoons should stay away."

"Sure they will," I said. "But when they don't, just remember that raccoons around here don't know the meaning of words like 'shoo' and 'scram.' Bud, up at the hardware store, runs a good business fixing door screens that raccoons have busted through, even when people are inside."

That evening one of the raccoons returned to see what Russell's van held in store. He sniffed the car but found no groceries, so he ambled up onto the deck to see if we had a screen door he could break through. But the glass slider was closed.

"Where is that stuffed raccoon?" I asked, looking for a toy that some child had left behind. It was about the size of a baby raccoon and had realistic markings. I put it on the deck and we waited.

The real raccoon approached with caution, taking one step in the direction of the odd-smelling relative, then pausing to wait for a reaction. I grabbed my camera and got a few pictures of the two nose-to-nose, just like seal moms bonding with their pups. Then the masked bandit ran off. We had a good laugh, imagining that the big rat went to hide because he didn't want the other raccoons to see how foolish he had been to fall for my trick.

48- Anne Chadwick

On bluff-top walks overlooking the Pacific, I have often seen an osprey perched in the cypress trees near the cormorants' nests. Sometimes his dark brown wings and white head make me do a double take, as I momentarily mistake him for a bald eagle, until I notice the trademark dark band of plumage across his eye. One morning I observed him fishing the adjacent cove in spectacular fashion. He soared about a hundred feet above the water, hovered when he spotted a fish, and then tucked his five-foot wings against his body for a steep dive. At the last second he flared his wings and plunged talons-first into the water, grabbing his prey with a death grip that he couldn't release until he landed on a solid surface. I've read that on some occasions an osprey will catch a fish so large that the bird is drawn underwater and drowns before he can let go.

After his dives, the osprey rose up from the water a safe distance, paused in midair, and gave a vigorous shake to get rid of excess water. He carried his catch back to the cypress trees for a quick meal before resuming the hunt. I did not see a nest by the ocean, although I have seen them on the Gualala River. Osprey nests are huge masses of sticks topping dead trees or snags, and the same nesting pair returns each year to the same spot.

There's a nest at Millerton Point on Tomales Bay that sits atop an old power pole. PG & E and the State Parks had the good sense to relocate the nest from an active power pole, and now an osprey pair returns safely to it each spring after a winter trip to Mexico. The pair incubates two or more eggs for five weeks and then feeds its chicks for nine weeks. The youngsters learn to feed on Tomales Bay and then join their parents on their annual journey to Mexico.

The osprey is a fairly common sight on the northern California coast, especially in spring and summer. The elimination of DDT improved its nesting success, just as it helped the brown pelican and countless other birds. There is still a danger the population will suffer from eating toxic fish, but one of the other threats is nearly gone. Egg collectors used to steal the ospreys' beautiful eggs from their nests. The eggs are buff white, spotted with shades of chocolate and lavender. Fortunately, egg snatching is no longer in vogue.

50- Anne Chadwick

Tree Dwellers

the sloped glass in an unsuccessful attempt to gain traction. It sprawled across the atrium, flapped its wings, slipped down the slope, and tumbled to the ground.

But I shouldn't sell the turkey short. A close look at the odd birds reveals amazing feathers of iridescent green, cooper, red, and bronze. Natives of the Southwestern United States and Mexico domesticated wild turkeys for their spectacular feathers long before the Pilgrims decided the large birds would make a tasty meal.

A less showy, shier tree dweller is the gray fox, the only member of the dog family in North America that climbs trees. It is not quite afraid of its own shadow, but almost. The fox will run for cover if a large bird flies over. A golden eagle can prey on young as well as adult foxes, for a mature animal weighs only six or eight pounds—a little less than my house cats. Probably, because the fox is a member of the *Canidae* family, people expect it to be a fearsome predator, but it only preys on mice, wood rats, snakes, and ground squirrels. Alan, one of my neighbors, circulated this e-mail about a fox in his yard:

"While we were enjoying the ocean from our living room window a few weekends ago, we witnessed a small, very fat fox. The fox ran by pursued by a young doe, with her head down as if to butt or challenge the fox. A few minutes later, back they raced the other way, the fox still chased by the deer. This occurred several more times before they vanished into the hedgerow. Surely the poor fox was thinking: *Wait a minute! Shouldn't this be the other way around? I should be chasing the deer!*"

Not nearly as elegant as the osprey are the wild turkeys I see roaming the chaparral. Like raccoons, the birds that patrol my neighborhood never seem affected by words like "shoo" and "scram." They are known to perch on people's car roofs and fight off would-be passengers. On one visit my brother, Bill, saw a few large, colorful turkeys alongside the road. He stopped, rolled down the window, and gobbled at them. They gobbled right back.

My friend, Sandy, told me they could fly pretty high—at least as high as the roof of her house. She and her husband, George, had added an atrium consisting of a glass roof sloping down to glass walls that enclosed a sun-drenched sitting room. One morning she got up at sunrise to check on an unfamiliar noise. It sounded like heavy footsteps across the top of the house, perhaps a prowler. She looked up just in time to see a four-foot turkey grasping at

52- Anne Chadwick

Wildflowers

Springtime signals renewal on the Pacific coast. Cormorants are busy feeding chicks in their impossibly perched nests. Redwoods come to life and send bright green growth shooting from the tips of darker branches. Whales pass by, with exuberant babies trying for the perfect breach.

Every meadow comes alive with wildflowers; it is nearly impossible to walk without stepping on a few. Rhododendrons put forth delicate pink blossoms that glow in the filtered light of redwood forests. Wild irises cover bluff tops with deep purple blooms on graceful green stalks. California poppies send their orange flowers in search of the sun, closing at night to reopen at daybreak. Massive mounds of blue lupines punctuated by red paintbrush create perfect rock gardens. My feet squish across succulents lining the cliffs.

Ice plant, sea fig, and seaside daisy produce a riot of red, pink, orange, and yellow blossoms on cliffs that make a spectacular foreground against azure waters beyond. Calla lilies soak up spring rain, and I take in the scent of wild roses that climb the stony gray wood of old sheds.

One morning when I went in search of the perfect rhododendron, it was a tiger lily that caught my eye. The flower seemed translucent in the morning light. Next to its fiery red flower were three buds in various stages of maturity, all drooping gracefully toward the forest floor. The elegant bulb provided one of the infinite surprises I have encountered on outings along the Pacific coast.

In Alaska, where spring arrives late, a field of fresh blooms can hold unexpected treats. One June afternoon on the Katmai Coast, I set out to photograph wildflowers in full swing, but incredulity silenced me when a brown bear and her cub approached over the crest. I sat motionless while they sauntered by just twenty yards above me, indifferent to my gape-jawed presence.

Fog

Fog can sneak up on a person. Carl Sandburg's poem, "Fog," says it comes on little cat feet, sits on silent haunches, and then moves on. There are days when the fog takes me by surprise.

My house sits on a redwood ridge about a half-mile inland and 500 feet above sea level, an altitude that normally puts me above the fog. On more than one sunny morning I have applied copious amounts of sunscreen, dressed in shorts and a tee shirt, and headed to the shore anticipating a warm walk on the beach. But, as I drive over the ridge crest and descend through tall trees toward the ocean, I see a dense marine layer shrouding the shore. I retreat to my house, don long pants and a sweater, and emerge again.

Dense fog creates a mysterious air, perhaps because it dampens the senses. Heavy mist reduces visibility, confuses sound, and can even put the taste of tiny, suspended salt particles in the air. Fog has caused many a shipwreck on the rugged Pacific coast. It can add to the danger and urgency of any situation, particularly those involving ships, trains, cars, and planes. Imagine the final scene of *Casablanca* without the fog; it just wouldn't be the same.

But a cool mist can also have a calming effect, especially if one is on foot. The movement of time seems to shift into slow motion. The wind rarely blows and colors are muted. Moisture buffers the sound of waves hitting rocks, and muffles the shrill cries of an oystercatcher announcing his approach for landing.

On the Pacific coast a dense summer fog usually indicates high temperatures inland. The contrast amazes me. One July afternoon I huddled by the fire, trying to warm up after a bone-chilling outing in the fog. A friend called from Sacramento, about one hundred miles inland, to recommend that I avoid the valley for a few days. "The temperature is hovering right around 115," he warned. I put on another sweatshirt, rubbed my hands by the fire, and thanked him for the advice.

58- Anne Chadwick

California Sea Lions

I walked to a harbor seal rookery on the northern Sonoma coast late one afternoon to see whether any new pups had arrived. At the south end of the rocks a small, different-looking seal perched on the edge and gazed out to sea. Her fur was brown and her body was sleeker than the others. When she turned to look at me I noticed a pointed nose and small earflaps, and she stood high on her front flippers. She was a sea lion pup, unrelated to the harbor seals that dominate this segment of the coast. I grew concerned about the young pup, who seemed to be searching for her mother. I could only hope she was not orphaned or abandoned. She flopped across the sharp rocks and approached the harbor seals, but they opened their toothy jaws in a display of aggression, warning her to keep her distance.

The pup's mother had probably parked her on the rocks while she went out hunting. But it was odd to see a lone sea lion pup in a harbor seal rookery. Normally, sea lions congregate in large colonies, and they behave totally unlike the quiet harbor seals.

California sea lions communicate by barking, and, having lost a few nights' sleep within auditory range of a colony, I can vouch that their volume and persistence are impressive. Males establish breeding territories on beaches each spring, and they vocalize almost nonstop to protect their harems from competing males. The females bark, as well. In a crowded sea lion colony, a mother and pup recognize each other by vocalization and scent. Sea lions think nothing of charging right over each other to get from one place to another. Harbor seals, in contrast, rarely touch each other, and only the infant pups vocalize.

Male sea lions, which get much larger than females and develop distinctive high foreheads, grow to imposing size. Their length sometimes exceeds eight feet, and their chests become massive. Adult males weigh between 400 and 800 pounds. They are the fastest of the aquatic carnivores, going up to twenty-five miles per hour. I enjoy the sight of sea lions swimming by in groups of three or four, just past the cresting waves. Their movement looks almost like dolphins', but the binoculars reveal squared foreheads and sleek brown bodies. Other times they rest in shallow waters, floating in a raft, each extending one flipper straight up into the air. The theory is that the flipper doubles as their air-conditioning system.

Morning Dew

The sun's first rays danced on only the highest tips of towering redwoods, casting an orange glow on dew-covered needles. Gradually, almost imperceptibly, the sky took on a sapphire hue, and morning shadows slanted sharply through the waking giants.

That February morning dawned clear and crisp, and I ventured out early to see whether my favorite field of calla lilies had begun to flower. A Sea Ranch meadow supported hundreds of calla lilies each spring, and by mid-February dozens of graceful white flowers erupted from broad green leaves. Spring seemed premature that year, and bold bloomers sent up tender shoots, oblivious to the threat of hard frosts before warmer weather arrived for good.

I felt the sun warm my back as I approached the tall white flowers for a closer look. A perfect stillness graced the morning air. Daybreak created a magical atmosphere for photographing the early upwelling of spring. Growing light approached from a low angle, producing strong shadows that emphasized the depth of each flower.

A single drop of dew hung on the tip of every calla lily that morning. By standing at just the right angle, I was able to catch a glimpse of the sun bursting through each individual drop of the dawn's dampness.

Alaskan Brown Bears

Until I went to Alaska, I had no idea how brown bears—also known as grizzlies—could be so varied in color, size, behavior, and disposition. For a precious week I was privileged to observe them in their totally wild habitat along the Pacific's Katmai Coast, eating, sleeping, mating, nursing, exploring, and even swimming. I was with eight other people, and we did not see another person for several days while we came very near these enormous bears in their beautiful country. This population of bears has never faced urban conflict—never been chased out of someone's garbage bins, never been accused of theft when a careless camper left food within reach—and as a result their reaction to humans is calm, a bit timid, and always curious.

We observed several mothers with two or three yearling cubs, and without fail, the cubs displayed contrasting dispositions. One cub would stick close to its mother, never straying more than a few feet from the sow and often getting literally underfoot. Another cub would exhibit a great sense of adventure and curiosity, roaming far from its mother and sticking its nose into every nook and cranny. Another might appear playful, tussling with a piece of

bull kelp or starting a game of tug of war with its sibling.

In early June the bears of Katmai spent most of their time foraging or sleeping. The salmon were not yet running in the area, so the bears bulked up on grasses, clams, barnacles, and the occasional fish. We often saw them grazing in tall sedge grasses, a beautiful pastoral scene with dramatic snow-capped mountains as a backdrop. Later in the year they would feast on salmon, adding to their weight before winter.

We arrived on one beach, knowing that a sow and two cubs were in the adjacent cove, so we waited and made no noise for a long time, hoping that they would wander our way. An adventuresome cub was the first to appear over the knoll separating the two coves, and then the mother and a more dependent cub followed, grazing on diverse vegetation all the while. I have no idea how long we stood and watched, since my sense of time evaporated under the spell of these magnificent animals. The three bears meandered down the hill toward us, and eventually the sow stood only twenty-five feet from me. I heard her sniff the air to explore my scent. Her ears came forward in a display of curiosity and she fixed her gaze on me. My heart pounded and I truly had to remind myself to breathe.

Our guide decided that the sow had come as close as safety would allow, so he spoke quietly to her in even tones and she made a small retreat before she resumed foraging. Toward the end of our encounter, the more adventuresome, curious cub sat up on his hind legs. He lifted his front paws in front of him, first to the left, then right, then left again, lifting them higher until, in one balletic move, he stretched straight up, stood erect, and waved his paws high above his head. It was then that I first saw the amazing detail of a brown bear's front feet, with articulated toes that enabled remarkable deftness.

The bears used that tremendous dexterity to eat clams at low tide. We watched one mother teach her more dependent cub to dig for clams. It appeared that she rejected his pleas to nurse, leaving him hungry and therefore more anxious to learn the art of clam digging. The large sow sniffed the sand at low tide, moving her nose across the ground like a metal detector, until she located a delicacy below. Then she dug into the sand to find the clam and bring it to the surface.

64- Anne Chadwick

The next move involved pressing down on the shell with terrific pressure, while twisting until it cracked open. Once the shell was split, the bear used her claws with great precision to pull apart the two halves and gain access to the meat inside. The cub paid close attention and waited eagerly for his mother to open a clam for him, as she ate some herself and left others for the youngster.

His more adventuresome sibling roamed the shore and found a few things to eat along the way. When I saw the lone cub out on a small spit that

reached into the sea, I thought it so strange to see a bear in a seascape where I normally would see a harbor seal in my native California. In fact, before humans intentionally exterminated brown bears and destroyed their habitat, California's coast must have been covered with cubs exploring rocky points dotted with sea stars and barnacles.

66- Anne Chadwick

Raising Bear Cubs

I could not believe my ears when I first heard the sound of bear cubs nursing. They make a steady noise like a small motor, or like kittens purring—magnified about a thousand times. Before they nurse, the cubs become very excited, bawling plaintive cries and hounding the mother. When she does let them nurse, she lies on her back and cradles them with her front legs. The scene evoked in me a great feeling of tenderness and devotion. I will never forget the sight of one satisfied cub after nursing, ready to explore the world with his full tummy and milk mustache.

Mother bears are typically so protective of their cubs that they will sacrifice their own safety for the sake of their youngsters. I watched one mother and her lone cub scramble up a steep cliff, seeking safe haven from an approaching boar. Although infanticide in bears may be uncommon, it does occur, and adult females and their cubs are always on guard when another bear approaches. The sow and cub sat on a rocky ledge while the boar passed by on the beach below, and the nervous pair never took their eyes off him. They stayed in their lofty hideout until long after he disappeared, and only then did they descend the rocky face with amazing agility and grace.

Storms

A strong storm blowing off the Pacific will send the heartiest souls running for cover. Even in the safety of my house on the Sonoma coast, my cats seek additional protection from a good squall by hiding deep under the bed. I don't blame them. The rain, wind, and hail pounding on windows and skylights remind me of riding through the carwash as a kid.

Redwoods bend in the wind, their branches sagging under the weight of unrelenting torrents. The ground at their feet grows moist, then wet, then saturated, and streams of runoff begin. Gravity pulls water toward the ocean, and temporary waterfalls pour from thirty-foot cliffs into the raging sea below.

Storms churn up the ocean, creating enormous waves that crash high over rocky shores. The roiling water tosses full-sized logs like toothpicks. Shorebirds hunker down, and seals head to the open sea to ride out the storm, safe from crushing waves on sharp rocks. When the sun breaks through after a storm its dramatic light bounces off receding thunderheads and still-tempestuous seas. New moisture intensifies the scents of fallen leaves, fresh grass, pungent soil, and the salty sea. The sheer size and power of a Pacific storm humbles a mere human like me.

Orcas

There is more to sunsets than the light show. Sounds and smells dance amid the fading light. I inhale the earthy scents—fresh grass, wildflowers, sea air. If I'm lucky, I hear a gray whale exhale as it breaks the surface, steady on its long journey from Mexico to Alaska, with a calf playing catch-up.

The sound of a whale's blow takes me back to the night when I was on San Juan Island in Washington State, driving back from a late dinner, nearly midnight. I pulled off the road to admire the stars. Right below the bluff a pod of orcas passed by in the inky black sea. It was too dark to see them, but their powerful blows let my ears track their movement southward along the shore. They sounded so close I imagined their spray might land on my face. That was one of my better whale-listening experiences.

In September 2002 I spotted two orcas patrolling the waters just off the Mendocino Headlands. Enormous, straight dorsal fins indicated they were both male. When I asked my local friends about it, they said that as kids thirty years ago they had seen orcas off the Mendocino coast all the time, a common sight. The last couple of decades, however, the killer whales went elsewhere, probably in search of salmon and trout. My friends, both volunteer leaders for the Gualala River Steelhead Project, took the orcas' return as a good sign that the steelhead population might be on the mend.

The following February a local biologist, also a volunteer for the state's largest fish-rescue project, was thrilled to report that a pod of at least a dozen orcas lingered close to shore, inside a protective reef where he had never before seen them. I was lucky enough to observe them from Black Point in March, a group of about fifteen whales, old and young, male and female.

They are sometimes called wolves of the sea because they hunt in packs and have a reputation as fierce carnivores. I've heard it said that in the ocean there are two types of creatures—orcas and orca food. They can take down a much larger whale with a coordinated hunt in which some orcas attack the pectoral fins, some go for the tail, and others aim for the head.

Watching them from the shore, I see only their grace and power. On the rare occasion when one hurls itself up out of the water, I catch a glimpse of its intriguing black-and-white markings. Perhaps there will be more chances to see them in coming years if we continue to restore our delicate rivers and bring back the salmon's precarious spawning grounds.

Tundra Swans

On any winter day the traveler who winds along Highway One north of Point Arena descends toward a field full of big white birds. *Really* big white birds. More than 200 tundra swans spend their winters in the Garcia Flats, a flood plain that becomes a mecca for waterfowl each winter. Standing more than four feet tall, they are the largest waterfowl. A look through binoculars reveals that they dwarf the Canada geese that share the field. I've stood next to Canada geese, even been chased by them, and they are good-sized birds. From a distance, tundra swans make them look a tad bigger than hummingbirds.

Many of the swans that I saw from the roadside one February morning still had their immature colors, most notably ash-gray necks, indicating they were less than a year old. These youngsters had hatched the previous summer at the northern reaches of Alaska, on its barren arctic coast. By October they had joined their flock in V-formation to fly an amazing distance south to this marshy field, where they spent the entire winter picking their way back and forth across tender grasses. The immature swans would molt before they left California, appearing snowy white by spring.

As I resumed my slow, curvy drive, I contemplated the contrast between the swans' journey and mine. Soon the huge white birds would be back on the Pacific flyway, graceful and efficient in their straight and steady flight. Their high-pitched yodeling and whooping would herald their return to northern nesting grounds. I, on the other hand, would hum along with old jazz standards on the stereo, slow to navigate sharp curves, keeping an eye out for the next fueling station.

Whimbrels and Black Turnstones

Sharing the Pacific flyway with the tundra swans are the whimbrel and black turnstone. I happened upon both birds one January morning on the Monterey Peninsula, sunning on the rocky shores of Pacific Grove. The whimbrel, which looks a lot like a long-billed curlew but for the dark stripe across its eye, nests in the Alaskan tundra each summer. Its long, curved bill is the perfect tool for probing the mud flats and rocky shores where it feeds all winter.

Black turnstones, small and slate-colored, also breed in coastal Alaska and fly as far south as Mexico for the winter. Maybe I was just hungry when I watched them, but I could have sworn their white-tipped feathers, dark-spotted chests, and milky white bellies looked like cookies and cream.

74 Anne Chadwick

Steller Sea Lions

It's hard to describe Steller sea lions without giving the impression of exaggeration. To say that they are the largest of all eared seals, or that they are three to four times as big as California sea lions doesn't do them justice. To describe their vocalizations as roars seems an understatement, as an active colony emits a cacophony of aggressive sounds in apparently endless battles for territory. A large male's enormous neck muscles, tremendous girth, bulging eyes, ferocious teeth, and loud roars make it a great candidate for the leading role in a sea-monster movie.

A male Steller sea lion can grow up to eleven feet long and weigh up to 2,400 pounds. Females are much smaller, weighing up to 770 pounds, and the difference in size accentuates the enormity of the males. I watched a huge bull emerge from the sea onto a rocky outcropping, and all the sea lions nearby scampered to higher ground or dove into the sea. His bulging neck muscles, emphasized by thick fur, gave him an intimidating stature. I could not believe the speed with which the frightened animals sought refuge from the sea monster by climbing to tremendous heights or diving off high cliffs into the water.

The Steller sea lions that inhabit America's Pacific coast, from Alaska through British Columbia and into a few spots along the California coast, are considered highly endangered. In fact, when I tried to view the population I had read about on Pt. Reyes, the ranger steered me clear of the delicate denizens, saying they were inaccessible. The American population was listed as threatened under the Endangered Species Act in 1990. Further study indicated that if the 1985–92 population trend continued, it was likely that sea lions would be extinct in Alaska from Prince William Sound westward within one hundred years. The decline has continued, and their status was worsened to "endangered" in 1997.

Principal threats are competition with fisheries, environmental change, predation by killer whales and sharks, disease, contaminants, and shooting by humans. I felt privileged to see a major Steller sea lion haul-out in Alaska, and I only hope these strange, magnificent beasts will be there to amaze and amuse future generations.

Monarch Butterflies

The first time I went to see monarch butterflies in their winter habitat, I was not impressed. Well, not for the first five minutes or so. George Washington Park in Pacific Grove was dotted with eucalyptus and pine trees whose leaves were dying, and I wondered where the colorful butterflies were hiding. Then I realized that the trees' dead leaves were not leaves at all, but the tan-and-black undersides of the butterflies' closed wings.

I could see my breath in the cold damp air of that early morning, a good indication that it was too cold for the butterflies to fly. They sat motionless in perfectly camouflaged clumps. Their numbers were overwhelming.

I now know that a sunny winter afternoon is the best time to see butterflies on the Monterey Peninsula. That's when the spectacular insects open their contrasting black, white, and orange wings. Some rest, wings open, on pine boughs or eucalyptus bark, while others fly overhead.

Their migration is a baffling intergenerational journey covering 2,000 miles. Unlike a gray whale, which returns to its birthplace each year, the migrating monarch has never been to its destination before. Several generations of monarchs have lived and died since last year's butterflies departed. Yet one butterfly's descendants return to the same grove—often the same specific tree—year after year. It has to be pure instinct, but exactly how they do it is a mystery. Scientists think they rely on earth's magnetic field, the position of the sun, and the polarization of the sun's rays to find their way to a home they've never seen before.

Monarchs west of the Rockies migrate to locations on the central California coast, including Pacific Grove, Santa Cruz, and Pismo Beach. Their winter sites are

When they arrive in their winter habitat, they cluster in large masses to conserve heat. They take flight when the temperature exceeds fifty-five degrees, and return to their clusters well before evening. Knowing how they operate, I find the sight of thousands of monarchs in their special winter grove to be absolutely thrilling.

neither cold enough to kill them, nor so warm that they waste precious energy flying too much. Coastal pine and eucalyptus groves provide the right microclimate from October through February: proper humidity, light, shade, temperature, and protection from wind. Monarchs east of the Rockies fly all the way to the high mountains of central Mexico each winter.

In spring and summer the Pacific offspring spread out through California's Central Valley, into the Sierra Nevada, and northeast to the Rocky Mountains. Their lifespan is only about six weeks, during which time they emerge from eggs to larvae, to caterpillars that metamorphose into butterflies, which then feed on nectar, mate, and lay eggs. As many as five generations of monarchs may develop by fall, when a special generation is born. Members of this unique group live much longer, up to eight months. They travel as far as 2,000 miles to their overwintering grounds, flying up to one hundred miles a day.

78- Anne Chadwick

Diving Birds

neck make him stand out. The female, in contrast, is brown with a few white patches and a decidedly dull gray bill.

These species are among the many diving birds that grace the Pacific coast. I know they're not really camera shy, but I could swear they duck underwater the minute I get set to release the shutter.

It's a well-known fact that male birds are far flashier than females, but the transformation they undergo to spruce up for breeding season is truly remarkable. The eye of the common loon, for instance, turns a striking red during breeding, a fabulous contrast to his iridescent green crown. His bill changes from gray to black, and he produces a yodeling call that would impress even the coolest female.

The horned grebe evolves from a simple gray-and-white affair to a handsome fellow with a chestnut chest, golden "horns," and a black-and-red face. His cousin, the eared grebe, develops spiky plumage for "ears," fanning out behind the eye.

Male surf scoters, which migrate from Alaska's tundra to California's coastal waters each winter, sport a colorful bill year round. The male's black plumage sets off a white, orange, and red bill. White patches on the forehead and back of his

Tule and Roosevelt Elk

"Delicate" is the word that comes to mind when I think of tule elk. It describes both their features and their place in the world. This diminutive subspecies of North American elk, which occurs only in California, is recovering well from near extinction. Frightfully near extinction. The current population of more than 3,000 stems from fewer than ten animals that were discovered and protected in 1874 in the southern San Joaquin Valley.

Until the Gold Rush, as many as 500,000 tule elk roamed central and coastal California. But in the mid-1800s, hunting and conversion of habitat to agriculture nearly obliterated them. In 1874, four years after the last known sighting, ranch workers discovered several tule elk while draining a marsh to create agricultural fields. The landowner, Henry Miller, chose to protect the animals, and by 1905 the population had grown to 140. He relocated many of them to other areas of California when his conservation program became so successful that the critters began to trample his fences and devastate his crops.

California's changing landscape and enormous human population make it impossible that the tule elk will ever return to their historic numbers or range, but I take great delight in seeing them thrive under recent restoration efforts. I've been lucky enough to see two of the subspecies' twenty-two herds around the state, and I'm relieved to know that the population is the highest it has been in 130 years. The largest herd, about 500 strong, roams Tomales Point, the spectacular peninsula at the north end of Point Reyes National Seashore. I ventured out to see them one spring day in 2003, and found them grazing in fields of lush grass and wild iris overlooking the Pacific. I spent a bucolic afternoon with that beautiful herd, amazed that it had grown from just ten animals that were reintroduced to the area in 1978. In the early years they languished under drought conditions, but now park officials have begun to relocate some of the herd to other areas of their historic range.

Individuals in the Tomales Point herd looked a bit bigger than deer, with sweet faces and enormous doe eyes. But I did not encounter any large bulls, which are much more imposing than females. A mature male's antlers can weigh up to forty pounds. An impressive rack of antlers comes in handy to intimidate younger bulls who might compete for the chance to breed. A dominant bull defends a harem of up to thirty females, and the secondary bulls may miss out on mating altogether. Most breeding is accomplished by just 10 percent of the male population.

Several months later, on a crisp October day in Redwood National Park, I encountered the largest subspecies of North American elk. What a contrast to the tule elk! A massive bull herded his harem into a meadow and then plopped down in the middle for a rest. He displayed one of the many uses for his enormous rack: when he titled his head back, the tip of his antlers reached just far enough to scratch his rump.

This subspecies flourished in the early 1800s along the Pacific coast from California to British Columbia. In fact, the Lewis and Clark expedition, fed up with salmon, feasted on elk during their dreary winter at Fort Clatsop in Oregon. By the mid 1800s, unregulated hunting for meat, hides and teeth (valued as ornamental accessories) severely depleted the population. In 1912, only 126 of these animals remained, and Theodore Roosevelt led efforts to save them.

Today, the largest population of Roosevelt elk thrives in Washington's Olympic National Park, which owes its origins to the elk conservation movement.

Gualala River

Among the many rivers that flow into the Pacific Ocean, the Gualala is the one with which I am most familiar. The river's wildlife and rugged beauty thrill me, but my visits there also stir sadness for what has been lost. Its source is high in the coastal range watershed, and its main forks run along the San Andreas fault line through Sonoma and Mendocino Counties. The thirty-two-mile river meanders through 190,000 acres of lush redwood and fir forest.

On hikes and kayak trips through this magnificent watershed, I have caught glimpses of ospreys, herons, red-tailed hawks, pelicans, belted kingfishers, killdeer, mergansers, and more. I have paddled near river otters, watched bats skim the river for bugs under the light of the full moon, and spied deer in the dense undergrowth. Friends who live in the area have also seen mink, bears, turtles, mountain lions, golden eagles, and spotted owls.

The river at one time was known internationally for its fishing, but one hundred years of logging have driven it to

"impaired" status under the federal Clean Water Act and nearly eliminated the population of coho salmon that once thrived. Sediment has filled in many of the river's deep pools that used to shelter salmon. Now, because the river is shallower and has less shade, it gets too hot to support the steelhead and coho. Each summer the Gualala chokes down to a mere trickle, and a hiker can hop across what once was a viable river.

Local volunteers and government officials are working to restore the river, but it's an uphill battle. I've spent a few days helping friends who run the Gualala River Steelhead

Project, the state's largest fish-rescue effort. One fall day when the flow rose after a hard rain, we released hundreds of steelhead trout and a few coho salmon that had survived summer in the project's holding ponds.

We loaded buckets of fish into the backs of pickup trucks and vans and headed to the river. I rode with the orga-nization's president, who had the honor of escorting the coho salmon. "This is the first time I've ever transported an endangered species," I told Roger with a wide grin. "It's kind of a thrill!"

Bald Eagles

Life for a young bald eagle is challenging, to say the least. For starters, an older chick might kill a younger one in the nest, and the parents would not intervene. Then, up to 40 percent of first flights are fatal. If a young eagle survives its journey out of the nest, it has about a 50 percent chance of starving during its first year because it cannot compete with more mature rivals for food. And yet the bald eagle is one of the fistful of success stories in recovery from endangered species status.

Before getting legal protection in the mid-1970s, America's great national symbol was driven to the brink of extinction by a combination of pesticides, hunting, loss of habitat, and lead poisoning that came from eating game wounded or killed by hunters' bullets. The world population has recovered to about 70,000, with more than half living in Alaska and about 20,000 in British Columbia. They flourish in the Pacific Northwest because of the abundant salmon population.

During my first day or two on Alaska's Katmai Coast

the sight of a bald eagle sent my spirits soaring, but as the week went on I became jaded. Soon bald eagles seemed as ubiquitous as seagulls along the California coast. In one cove I spotted at least a dozen in each panorama—nesting, fishing, soaring, or resting on high branches and cliffs. I watched one eagle swoop down from a tree branch and fly over a brown bear and her cubs, and then sail away on invisible air currents. When he passed over the bears

I realized how enormous he was, with a wing-span exceeding seven feet. Only when his wings reached clear across the resting bear family did I appreciate, in perspective, the immense size of the eagle.

Bald eagles use their enormous wings to soar with minimal effort. One morning, from a vantage point high atop San Juan Island, I watched a bald eagle rise up about 1,000 feet without flapping its wings. It found a thermal and spread its wings to their full span. Banking left or right but never pumping its wings, the eagle spiraled upward in a rapid climb that quickly put it well above the island's highest peaks. Eagles can migrate at an average speed of thirty miles per hour with little effort, going long distances by climbing high in a thermal, then gliding downward to catch the next thermal, and the next. Several eagles soaring together in a thermal are called a "kettle of eagles."

These magnificent birds are known for their eyesight. They have eyelids that close when they sleep, but when they're awake a second eyelid blinks to clean their eyes. Every three or four seconds, a membrane slides across the cornea to clear dirt and dust, and because it's translucent, eagles can see during mid-blink. Once a bald eagle spots a fish near the water's surface, it approaches its prey in a shallow glide and grabs it with a quick swipe of its talons. Like osprey, their talons lock on their catch and cannot open again until the eagle pushes down on a solid surface. Occasionally, a bald eagle plunges into the water while trying to catch a fish. The eagle cannot fly with wet wings, so it swims to shore, propelled by its soggy wings. They are strong swimmers, but some succumb to hypothermia. When I noticed a bald eagle drying its wings after a swim, it reminded me of a cormorant pausing for the dry cycle after diving for fish.

Sunsets

My theory about sunsets is that, like snowflakes, no two are alike. I wish I had the time to sit and watch them all, just to prove my premise. My favorite spots for spying sunsets are along the northern California coast's protected cliffs, just below bluff level, sheltered from the wind. Spring evenings there can be brisk, or downright cold when there's a stiff breeze. I can sit by the ocean for hours, bundled and binoculared, while the earth rotates imperceptibly from day into night. The setting sun melts the steel blue Pacific and ignites clouds aloft. Tide pools light up like molten lava.

Friends of mine have seen the elusive green flash that sometimes follows a sunset over the ocean. I have never witnessed it, and for a long time I suspected it was an optical illusion, a result of staring at the red sun until it disappeared and left its complementary color, green, in its absence. But then I saw an amazing photograph by A. J. Wool that captured the green flash on film. Perhaps someday my eyes will take it in.

As the sun sets over the Pacific, oystercatchers skim the water, bright orange beaks reflecting the last rays of sun. Their noisy cries fill the salt air. Harbor dolphins cruise by, moving like small whales just past the cresting waves. They break the surface in serene and steady style, small blows announcing their rhythmic presence.

If it's low tide, harbor seals bask on the rocks and soak up the day's remaining rays. A high tide tells them its time to abandon the shore in search of food.

And I go on watching sunsets, listening for a whale's blow, gasping at the power of waves against rocks, and hoping to see the green flash. So far my observations have confirmed my theory that each sunset is wonderfully unique.

Pacific in My Soul - 87

Acknowledgments & Credits

I have many people to thank for helping this work come to fruition. I appreciate the support and encouragement of my brothers, Glenn, Bill, and John, with special thanks to Bill for the Baja whale picture and for his good company on that trip. I thank Jenny Ross for introducing me to the magnificent brown bears of Alaska and coaching me in the art of photography. Janice Cooper's faith in me as a writer and photographer, as well as her meticulous editing, were invaluable. My niece Becky played an important role as reader and number-one fan, and the feeling is mutual. Roger Dingman expanded my world to include the glorious Gualala River watershed and all its hidden treasures. Olga and Henry Carlisle provided inspiration and encouragement, not to mention the sanctum of St. Pantaleon. Trever Barker patiently gave me pointers in the complex fields of graphic design and printing. When

Malcolm Margolin looked at an early draft and said, "This is a *real* book," his words fueled the perseverance that proved essential. I appreciate the sound guidance and hard work of all the people at Cypress House. I thank my dad, Jim Chadwick, for his unwavering support of my photography habit. And I have to express the deepest appreciation for my mom, Dorothy, who gave me the soul that cherishes it all.